MW00586224

SOFTWARE DESIGN DECODED

The MIT Press
Cambridge, Massachusetts
London, England

SOFTWARE DESIGN
DECODED

66 Ways Experts Think

Marian Petre and André van der Hoek

Illustrations by Yen Quach

This book was set in Milo by the MIT Press. Printed and bound in the United
States of America.

Library of Congress Cataloging-in-Publication Data

Names: Petre, Marian, 1959– author. | Hoek, André van der, 1971– author. |
    Quach, Yen, 1992– author.
Title: Software design decoded : 66 ways experts think / Marian Petre, André
    van der Hoek, and Yen Quach.
Description: Cambridge, MA : The MIT Press, [2016]
Identifiers: LCCN 2016008329 | ISBN 9780262035187 (hardcover : alk. paper)
Subjects: LCSH: Computer software--Human factors--Popular works. | Computer
    software--Development--Popular works.
Classification: LCC QA76.76.H85 P48 2016 | DDC 005.1--dc23 LC record available
    at https://lccn.loc.gov/2016008329

10   9   8   7   6   5   4   3

For more information and background about the book,
as well as additional insights contributed by the community,
see https://mitpress.mit.edu/software-design-decoded

PREFACE

What makes an expert software designer? The typical answer—experience and innate ability—is less than satisfying. While it carries elements of truth, it offers little from which we can learn and generalize. Experts clearly do not just approach their work randomly. Quite the contrary, they have specific habits, learned practices, and observed principles that they employ deliberately during their design work.

This book offers a look at those habits, practices, and principles, one rooted in many years of studying professional software designers and their ways of working. It offers 66 "things that expert software designers do," each of which can be traced back to academic literature that documents expert behavior and each of which has been confirmed to us time and again by those working in the field.

Some may be familiar, others not. Some are easily put in practice, others not. Some have immediate impact, others not. A constant, however, is that expert software designers are keenly aware of *all* of these practices and draw on them when the situation calls for it.

Today, software is no longer limited by technology, but rather by imagination. Yet the software that turns the imagined into reality can be complex, and the context in which this transformation must happen can be even more complex. This places extraordinary demands on software designers, demands that can be met only if we collectively "step up" to achieve sustained excellence in design.

We hope this book plays its part.

ACKNOWLEDGMENTS

This book would not have been possible without the many software designers we have been able to study, observe, interview, and simply talk to over the years. We appreciate your generosity, and hope that you might still be able to find a practice or two to adopt. Our sincere gratitude.

In addition, we thank the following individuals for their contributions to the book: Alex Baker, Clive Baldwin, Gerald Bortis, Randi Cohen, Grace Petre Eastty, Max Petre Eastty, Peter Eastty, Thomas Green, Jasper Grimm, Uwe Grimm, Michael Jackson, Christopher Keller, Kimberly Keller, Crista Lopes, Consuelo Lopez, Tamara Lopez, Marie Lufkin Lee, Clara Mancini, Nick Mangano, Lee Martie, Martin Nally, Peter Petre, Edgar Weidema, Greg Wilson.

SOURCE NOTES
FOR ILLUSTRATIONS

3—Experts divide and conquer

Trygve Reenskaug (1979). Models - Views - Controllers, Xerox PARC Technical Note, December 10, 1979. Based on Tryvge Reenskaug, THING-MODEL-VIEW-EDITOR—an Example from a Planning System, Xerox PARC Technical Note, May 12, 1979. Available at http://heim.ifi.uio .no/~trygver/2007/MVC_Originals.pdf [Accessed June 15 2016].

6—Experts use metaphor

J. M. Carroll and C. Carrithers (1984). Training Wheels in a User Interface. *Communications of the ACM* 27 (8):800–806.

7—Experts prefer working with others

Used by permission, drawing based on photograph
from: A. van der Hoek and M. Petre, eds. (2013). *Software
Designers in Action: A Human-Centric Look at Design
Work*. CRC Press / Taylor & Francis Group, 452 pages.
ISBN 978-1-4665-0109-6.

10—Experts involve the user

Based on dog-appropriate switches designed by Clara
Mancini. http://www.open.ac.uk?blogs/ACI/.

13—Experts prefer solutions that they know work

R.T. Fielding and R.N. Taylor (2002). Principled Design
of the Modern Web Architecture. *ACM Transactions on
Internet Technology* 2 (2):407–416.

28—Experts invent notations

Example provided by Jasper Grimm, based on a notation developed by Jeff Walker: J. Walker (1982). Variations for Numbers Jugglers, *Juggler's World* 34 (1):11–14.

38—Experts address knowledge deficiencies

Based on *The Wizard of Oz*, 1939, Metro-Goldwyn-Mayer.

54—Experts test across representations

Used by permission, drawing based on photograph from A. van der Hoek and M. Petre, eds. (2013). *Software Designers in Action: A Human-Centric Look at Design Work*. CRC Press / Taylor & Francis Group, 452 pp. ISBN 978-1-4665-0109-6.

EXPERTS
KEEP IT
SIMPLE

EXPERTS PREFER SIMPLE SOLUTIONS

Every design problem has multiple, if not infinite, ways of solving it. Experts strongly prefer simpler solutions over more complex ones, for they know that such solutions are easier to understand and change in the future. Simplicity is so important to them that they often continue to search for simpler solutions even after they have a solution in hand.

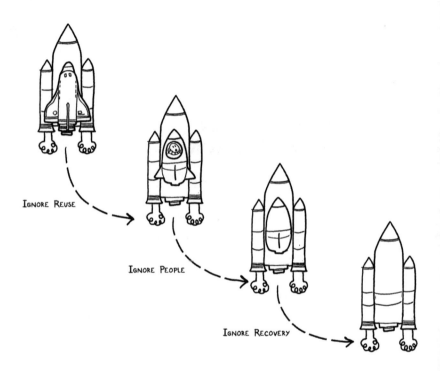

IGNORE REUSE

IGNORE PEOPLE

IGNORE RECOVERY

EXPERTS SOLVE SIMPLER PROBLEMS FIRST

Experts do not try to think about everything at once. When faced with a complex problem, experts often solve a simpler problem first, one that addresses the same core issue in a more straightforward form. In doing so, they can generate candidate solutions that are incomplete, but provide insight for solving the more complex problem that they actually have to solve.

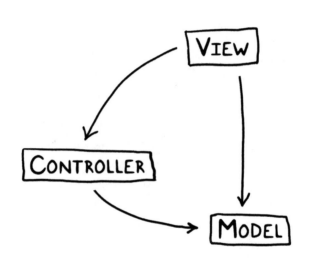

EXPERTS DIVIDE AND CONQUER

Experts know when and how to break down a complex problem into smaller problems that can be solved independently. In addressing the parts, however, they do not forget about the whole: they reflect on the relationships between parts. When what emerges in solving one part affects other parts, they make adjustments. Indeed, they sometimes repartition the whole problem and solution as a result.

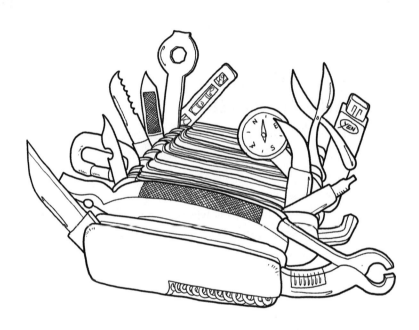

EXPERTS DO NOT OVERGENERALIZE

General solutions are preferred over less general solutions, both for the design as a whole and for its constituent parts. Experts, however, avoid *over*generalizing, which constitutes wasted effort and leads to solutions that are more complex than necessary. The balance is important. Experts use what they know about the practical constraints of the design context to decide whether to generalize for reuse or to optimize for the immediate situation.

```
$ls -l | grep "Jan" | sort +2n | more
```

5

EXPERTS DESIGN ELEGANT ABSTRACTIONS

While all developers create abstractions, experts *design* them. A good abstraction makes evident what is important, both in what it does and how it does it. Through a single lens, it communicates the problem it solves and the machinery of its solution.

Experts are not satisfied with just any abstraction, they deliberately seek elegant abstractions through which complex structures can be introduced, understood, and referred to efficiently.

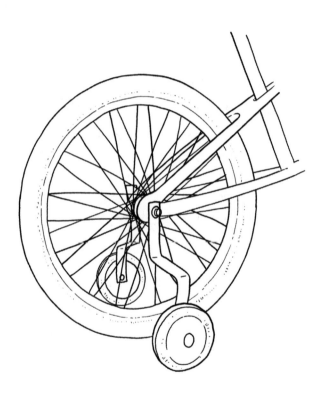

6

EXPERTS USE METAPHOR

Experts frequently use metaphor to discuss parts of a design and how it works. By invoking metaphor, a more vivid and immediately available picture is evoked of some aspects of the software, which particularly benefits collaborative design work in quickly and succinctly communicating ideas and assumptions.

EXPERTS
COLLABORATE

EXPERTS PREFER
WORKING WITH OTHERS

To experts, the image of the designer as a lone genius who has flashes of brilliance is a fallacy. Experts know that stimulation through working with others is key to their own design performance. Moments of surprising or deep insight do happen, but experts know that those moments are more likely in a rich, collaborative environment.

QUICK QUESTION ABOUT YOUR SECURITY MODULE

YEAH I CAN HELP

HOW DO I ADAPT FOR...

8

EXPERTS REACH OUT

Experts deliberately involve others outside of their team when they have a purpose for doing so, often to obtain specialized technical or domain knowledge. Experts do not wait to contact others when they need them; they know that "sooner is better."

EXPERTS CHECK
WITH OTHERS CONTINUALLY

Experts know to check with collaborators regularly
to coordinate mutual efforts, goals, ideas, and
assumptions. They know that individual work may
diverge within a collaboration, and that spotting
divergence is crucial, both to identifying errors and
seizing opportunities. Frequent ad hoc communication
(rather than formal meetings) is a feature of high-
performing teams.

EXPERTS INVOLVE THE USER

Experts are acutely aware of users. They deliberately involve users in the design process, studying them, talking to them, engaging them in testing intermediate designs, and even asking them to take an active role in the design team.

Yet experts do not take everything users say at face value. They realize the potential limitations, as users' thinking is often colored by current experiences. Experts look beyond what users ask for, to what users actually need.

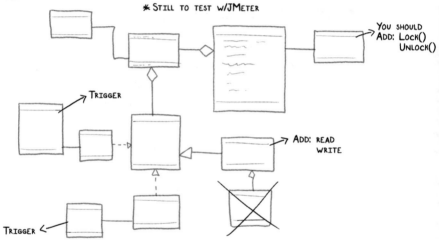

※ COOL DESIGN, SOME FLEXIBILITY NEEDED THOUGH

※ STILL TO TEST W/JMETER

YOU SHOULD
ADD: LOCK()
UNLOCK()

TRIGGER

ADD: READ
WRITE

TRIGGER

※ TRIGGERS SHOULD USE OBSERVER PATTERN

EXPERTS SOCIALLY EMBED AND REINFORCE GOOD PRACTICE

11

Experts know that the interplay between designers plays a crucial part both in nurturing creativity and in promoting quality and rigor. They consciously embed and reinforce good practice in their team. They use knowledge of the group, of both individual and combined strengths and limitations, to structure activities, provide systematic checks, and share knowledge. This collective safety net liberates individuals to extend themselves.

Experts especially take care over the induction of new members into local culture and practice, while eliciting fresh perspectives from them.

12

EXPERTS AGREE
TO DISAGREE

For the benefit of the design project, experts often
agree to disagree. They know that divergence of
opinions can drive innovation and excellence in design.
They also know that many decisions made early
are adjusted, retracted, or refined later on, and so
prolonged haggling tends to be counterproductive if
there is more design to do. Instead, experts accept
temporary disagreement and proceed in designing
other aspects of the project. More information resulting
from further design activity will help them resolve
their disagreement.

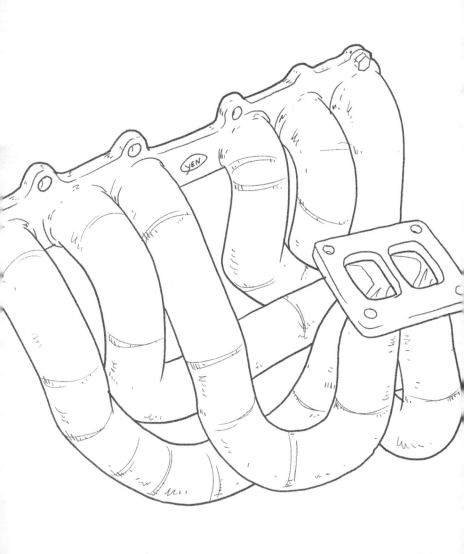

EXPERTS
BORROW

REST

13

EXPERTS PREFER SOLUTIONS THAT THEY KNOW WORK

Experts have no desire to "re-invent the wheel." If they have a solution that works, or know of one elsewhere, they will adopt that solution and move on to other parts of the design task. Of course, they know to re-assess the existing solution within the context of the current project, to make sure that it actually fits. As long as it does, and as long as it is legally and ethically allowed, they choose to borrow rather than build, reuse rather than re-implement, and copy rather than draft.

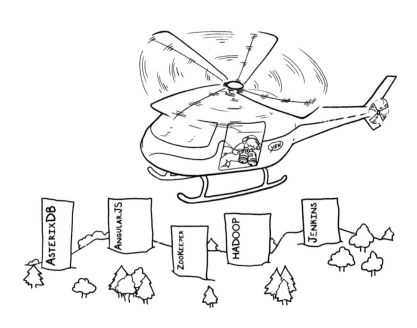

14

EXPERTS LOOK AROUND

In the same way that architects walk cities to examine
and take inspiration from existing buildings, software
experts examine the designs of other software to
"see how they did it." They frequently do so in response
to a particular challenge they face, but they often
also spend time looking around just to add to their
repertoire of possible design solutions to draw upon
in the future.

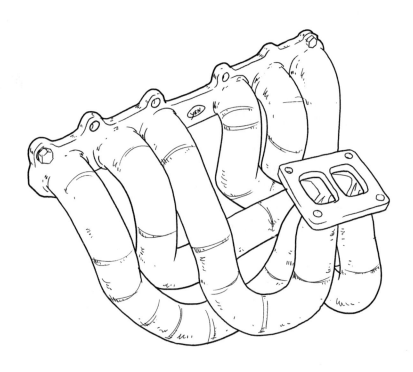

15

EXPERTS TAKE INSPIRATION FROM WHEREVER THEY CAN

Experts live with their heads up and their eyes open. They are aware of their surroundings and "try on" any ideas they spot. They take inspiration from other people, from other areas (photography, astronomy, literature, model railways), and from their wider environment (a whiteboard drawing, a blog post, a toy, a game). They continually collect ideas that might be useful.

16

EXPERTS USE ANALOGY

In dealing with intractable problems, experts sometimes turn to analogy, levering likeness and unlikeness to other situations to shift their thinking. They carefully examine where the analogy holds and where it does not, and especially use where it breaks down to drive their understanding of the design problem at hand.

ARCHITECT

Focus on security

Perfectionist

Programs essential,
most difficult parts

Knows code inside-out

NEWBIE

Focus on basic functionality

Fearful

Programs small bug fixes

Knows code barely

SENIOR PROGRAMMER

Focus on extensibility

Somewhat sloppy

Programs major new
features

Knows major parts well

RELEASE ENGINEER

Focus on stability

Detail-oriented

Programs patches

Acquainted with
most of the code

EXPERTS USE DESIGN METHODS (SELECTIVELY)

17

Experts do not re-invent how to go about design. While they know that design is a creative process that involves impromptu activities, they also use structured design methods to advance their project when appropriate.

They know of and apply a host of methods (world modeling, tradeoff analysis, refactoring, storyboarding, test-driven development, cognitive walkthrough). However, they also know the limitations of such methods and apply them only if they believe their project will benefit. Experts balance systematic practice with freedom of invention.

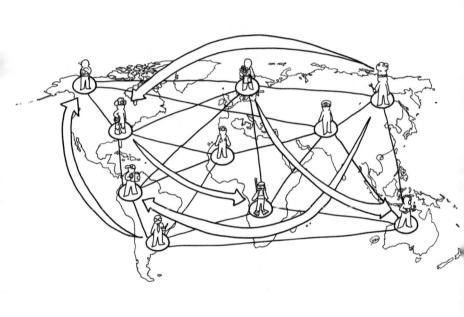

18

EXPERTS NETWORK

Experts are very aware that they do not know everything—far from it. They compensate by building a network of people who know things, have special expertise and domain knowledge, or know how to think and question. They know to whom to turn when they need something.

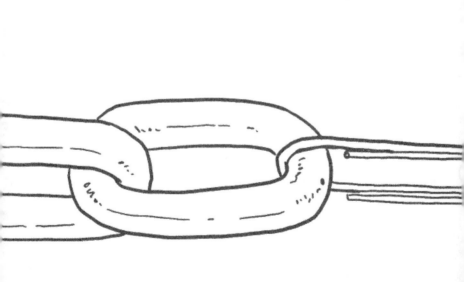

EXPERTS
BREAK
THE RULES

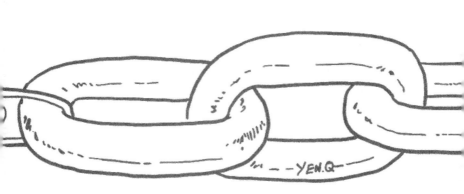

EXPERTS RELAX CONSTRAINTS

Experts do not take much for granted, and for tough problems they will reconsider just about anything, including hard constraints. They relax these constraints in order to explore a broader range of possibilities, sometimes relaxing different constraints successively so as to challenge their understanding and promote insight.

Experts particularly break constraints early, when creativity and exploration are needed. Of course, as they progress and begin to form a more comprehensive solution, they want clarity and completeness, and re-introduce the genuine constraints they previously ignored.

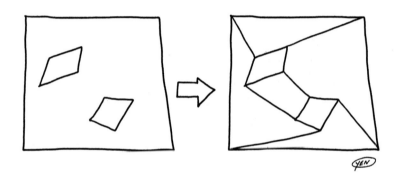

EXPERTS RESHAPE
THE PROBLEM SPACE

Experts often step back from the stated problem and consider the problem space more broadly, looking for alternative ways of understanding "what the problem is." They may change direction by reconceiving the problem space, or by addressing a different problem in the same space. They intentionally choose somewhat different goals from the original design problem, as this leads to insights either into where the real problem lies, or into how to overcome key obstacles.

EXPERTS USE NOTATIONS AS LENSES, RATHER THAN STRAIGHTJACKETS

21

Experts understand the true value of notations: they serve as lenses to examine a design problem or advance a design solution from a particular perspective. Experts are not married to any one notation and will use whichever notation best suits the task at hand.

As any notation emphasizes some information at the expense of other information, experts remember to complement the leverage a notation gives them with engaging with what is outside of it.

REQUIREMENTS DESIGN

INTERACTION DESIGN

ARCHITECTURE DESIGN

IMPLEMENTATION DESIGN

TIME

EXPERTS DESIGN THROUGHOUT THE CREATION OF SOFTWARE

22

Experts do not subscribe to the vision that design is merely a phase during which requirements are transformed into an architecture or implementation design. Rather, experts know that requirements are designed, that interactions are designed, that architectures are designed, that code is designed, and—most important—that all these forms of software design inter-relate and are often worked on in parallel. They know it is therefore frequently important to break out of a prescribed software development process and engage in design activities where and when necessary.

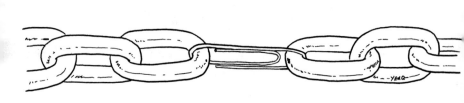

EXPERTS DO NOT FEEL OBLIGED TO USE THINGS AS INTENDED

23

Experts use what is useful to them and no more. Because they understand what they need and why, they adopt things on their own terms. They may apply a methodology selectively, recombine process steps, cross paradigms, alter model solutions, or use methods in unexpected ways.

EXPERTS
SKETCH

EXPERTS EXTERNALIZE THEIR THOUGHTS

Experts sketch when they think. They sketch when alone. They sketch in meetings with colleagues or clients. They sketch when they have no apparent need to sketch. They sketch on paper, on whiteboards, on napkins, in the air. Experts know that sketching is a way to interact with their own thoughts, an opportunity to externalize, examine, and advance what they have in their minds.

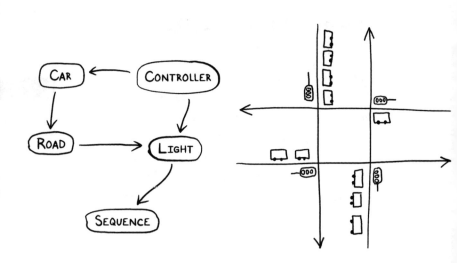

EXPERTS DRAW THE PROBLEM AS MUCH AS THEY DRAW THE SOLUTION

Experts know that their understanding of the design problem and their understanding of its solution inevitably deepen and co-evolve as they design. Experts therefore draw the problem as much as they draw the solution: by moving back-and-forth, they not only ensure that both stay in sync, but also explicitly use advances in the understanding of one to drive advances in the understanding of the other.

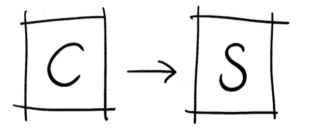

EXPERTS DRAW WHAT THEY NEED AND NO MORE

Experts are frugal in creating their sketches. Experts draw what they need to support their thinking, discussion, argument, communication, or other design activity—but no more. A sketch consisting of a few boxes, a few arrows, and a few annotations is not uncommon, as is a diagram that is later uninterpretable because of its sparseness. Providing detail when it is not needed is a waste of effort and distracts from the task at hand.

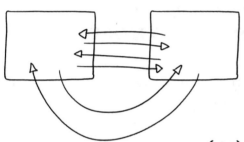

$$(s,t) \text{ Send } (s`,t`) <==>$$

$$(snt=\emptyset) \wedge (s`=\emptyset) \wedge$$

$$(t`=t \cup S)$$

EXPERTS SHIFT BETWEEN FORMAL AND INFORMAL

Experts are not lazy. When the situation calls for it, they employ much more formal diagrams than the sketches they typically create. To model certain phenomena more clearly—with more precision and completeness—they may well work out a state machine in all of its detail, edit pseudocode on a whiteboard, or meticulously specify all of the entities, fields, keys, and relationships in a database schema. Once done, however, they will quickly return to sketching, employing a more informal style that abandons much notational detail.

27

4 BALL
NOTE: ASYNCHRONOUS

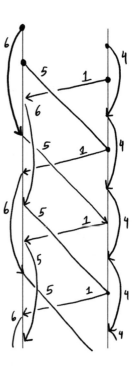

EXPERTS INVENT NOTATIONS

Experts choose a notation that suits the problem, even
if the notation does not exist. New notations arise
when, in the heat of design, shorthand symbols are
used that take on a meaning of their own. This meaning
typically persists for the duration of the design meeting,
but in some cases use of the symbols becomes more
pervasive in the design project.

28

EXPERTS KEEP SKETCHES

Experts prefer to keep their sketches rather than discard them. Their desks are cluttered with paper sketches. Their whiteboards are full of drawings. They may have an archive full of old sketches. All for a reason: they know they may need to revisit a sketch, whether to consult it to re-invigorate their understanding or to evolve it because some goal or constraint has changed.

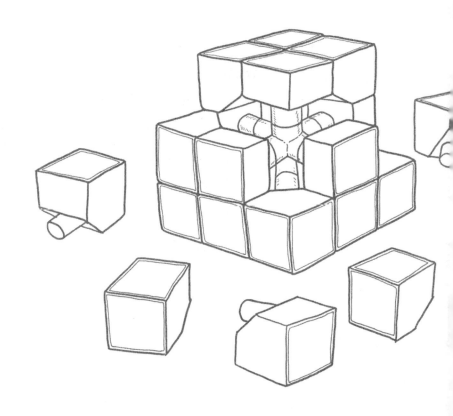

29

EXPERTS
WORK WITH
UNCERTAINTY

EXPERTS KEEP OPTIONS OPEN

Although a natural inclination might be to solidify any design decision that can be made as early as possible, experts do the opposite: they prefer to keep their options open. They know that any decision they make now may need to be revised later if they wish to explore an alternative direction. Therefore, if they do not have to make a particular decision yet, they simply will not make it.

30

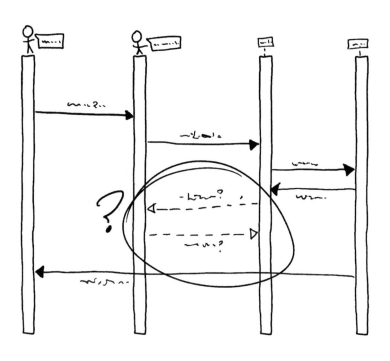

EXPERTS MAKE PROVISIONAL DECISIONS

To further a design solution, experts often make decisions provisionally. They keep track of which decisions are firm and which are provisional, as well as the conditions under which the decisions are made. This way, they acknowledge explicitly where their design is still tentative and where it is more definite.

31

EXPERTS SEE ERROR
AS OPPORTUNITY

Design regularly involves error: things that "go amiss,"
misunderstandings, obstacles, wrong turns, emergent
issues. Rather than fearing error, experts embrace error
as opportunity. They accept it as an inherent part of
design and take time to explore both the failure and
the context around it. Understanding what happened
often reveals insights about the problem—or about
the solution—such as assumptions, misconceptions,
misalignments, and emergent properties.

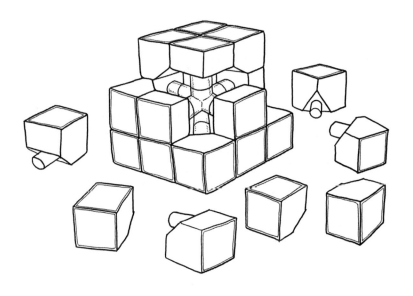

32

EXPERTS KNOW
HOW THINGS WORK

Experts have a huge, accessible store of knowledge.
They know how things work in general. They know
how specific things work. They know how the current
design works. When something is uncertain, experts
bring that knowledge to bear, extending from the
known to the unknown.

	DESIGN ALTERNATIVE 1	DESIGN ALTERNATIVE 2	DESIGN ALTERNATIVE 3
DEVELOPMENT TIME	****	**	******
COST OF ACQUIRING COTS COMPONENTS	******	***	****
REUSE OF OUR EXISTING CODEBASE	******	*******	****
COMPATIBILITY	******	****	*******
PERFORMANCE	******	******	*******
SECURITY	****	*******	****

EXPERTS MAKE TRADEOFFS

No design problem can be solved perfectly. Experts realize that designing is making tradeoffs, with each decision they make favoring some aspects of the design solution over others. Experts inform their decisions by collecting as much information as possible and considering how each potential decision trades off among their design goals.

34

EXPERTS PRIORITIZE AMONG STAKEHOLDERS

The history of software is littered with examples in which the wrong stakeholders were prioritized (usually managers over end users). Experts cut through issues of positions of power and human preference, opinion, and bias to identify the real stakeholders—the people who in the end determine whether or not the system will be adopted successfully. By focusing on them, experts can set the right design priorities for the project.

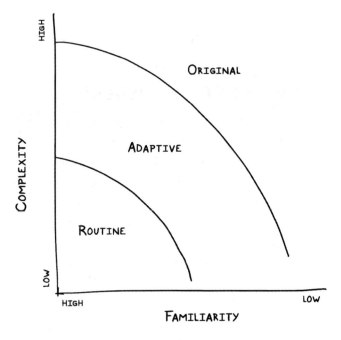

35

EXPERTS ADJUST TO THE DEGREE OF UNCERTAINTY PRESENT

Different design problems incur different amounts of uncertainty. Experts know which type of problem they are dealing with and adjust their practices accordingly. Routine problems have less uncertainty and are handled in a standard, informed manner, with many decisions made early. Adaptive and original problems involve more uncertainty and require exploration and invention. This entails maintaining more alternatives, deferring more decisions and making provisional decisions, and backtracking as necessary.

36

EXPERTS ARE NOT **AFRAID**

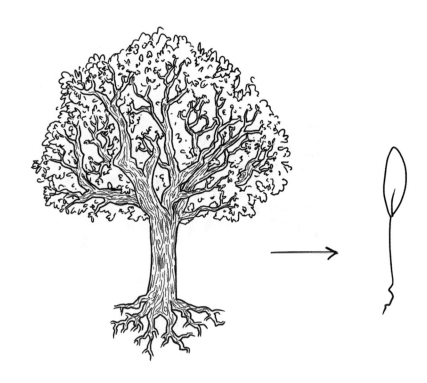

EXPERTS FOCUS ON THE ESSENCE

Every design problem has an essence, a core set of considerations that must be understood and "nailed" in the design solution for it to solve the problem successfully. This essence can be disruptive: changes in the core drastically alter the peripheral decisions that need to be made. Experts focus their efforts on the essence first, and delay expending effort designing on the periphery.

37

EXPERTS ADDRESS KNOWLEDGE DEFICIENCIES

Experts make every effort to find out and fill in what they do not know. In fact, experts explicitly look for gaps in their understanding of a design problem and its possible solutions, and they try to address those deficiencies as early as they can. They know that "not knowing" is worse than knowing that something is problematic.

A particular form of knowledge deficiency is assumptions. Experts know that making assumptions is an integral part of design practice, but make every effort to verify whether or not their assumptions hold.

EXPERTS GO
AS DEEP AS NEEDED

Experts are not afraid to get their hands dirty in nitty-gritty details. If code must be written to understand whether a particular algorithm is sufficiently performant, they write code. If model checking is needed to guarantee a certain property in their design, they build and check the model.

39

Experts know that any abstraction they make is eventually put to the test by its transition to code, which is why they often engage with implementation—even during conceptual design. Aligning abstraction and implementation enforces discipline and accuracy.

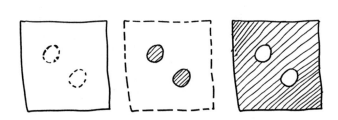

EXPERTS TRY
THE OPPOSITE

Experts take drastic measures when needed. When they
are stuck, they might try the opposite. This may not lead
to a satisfactory solution, but it almost certainly leads
to new insights that help them free their minds, identify
new possibilities, and decide on how to press forward.

EXPERTS DO SOMETHING (ELSE)

Most design projects bog down at some point, when every suggestion seems to lead to further problems. Rather than continuing to "bang their heads" against the same problem, experts switch their focus to another part of the design. It often does not matter what they choose to work on, as long as they change focus for a while. Doing so is likely to reveal considerations that help them overcome the obstacle.

EXPERTS KNOW WHEN TO STOP

Experts are sensitive to when the incremental benefits of revisiting the same issue diminish. They have a strong internal gauge as to when it is time to stop and move on.

42

DesignSketch = Box* + Relationship*

Box = Name Port*

Relationship = "("Box Box Arrow")"

Arrow = "⟶" | "⟵" | "⟷" | "⎯⎯"

Name = [a-zA-Z0-9]+

Port = ...

EXPERTS BUILD THEIR OWN TOOLS

Experts go to great lengths to surround themselves with the right tools for the job. This includes not only finding, evaluating, and appropriating external tools, but also creating special-purpose tools (intermediate languages, testing tools, visualizations) that fit the design situation.

43

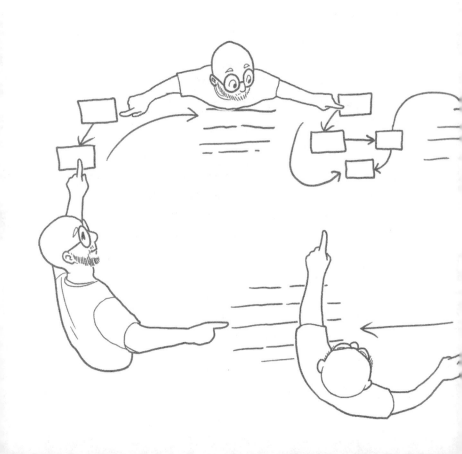

EXPERTS
ITERATE

EXPERTS REPEAT ACTIVITIES

Experts ask the same questions multiple times, of different people, but also of the same people. Experts test their designs, not once, but multiple times. Experts draw a diagram, then draw it again, and perhaps again and again. Experts repeat these activities because they know that, each time they do so, they must re-engage with a fresh mindset and re-explain to themselves or others. Variations in how they engage, think, draw, and communicate, as well as variations in what they choose to focus on, uncover new issues and opportunities.

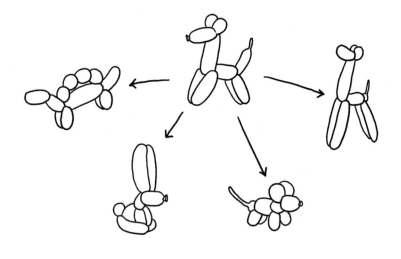

44

EXPERTS GENERATE ALTERNATIVES

Experts explicitly seek, develop, and evaluate alternatives throughout design. They do this at all levels. By probing these alternatives, even just in their minds, they maintain as much flexibility in the design solution as possible. Alternatives make explicit where and how the design might be able to "give" in the face of future decisions.

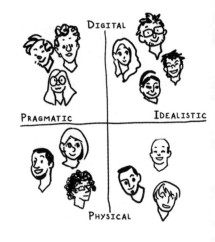

45

EXPERTS EXPLORE
DIFFERENT PERSPECTIVES

Experts examine a design problem, and its possible
solutions, from different perspectives. They examine
the problem from both a human and a technical
perspective. They assess architectures for their structural
quality, implementability, and deployability. They look
at both the usability and the accessibility of different
interface mock-ups. Because they know that focusing
narrowly on a single perspective is guaranteed to
miss important considerations, they explicitly iterate
over multiple perspectives.

46

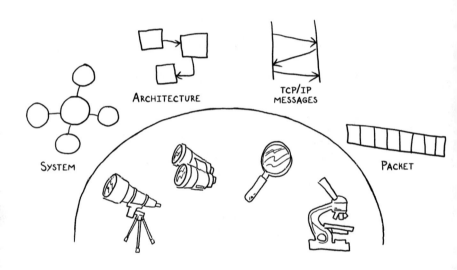

SYSTEM

ARCHITECTURE

TCP/IP
MESSAGES

PACKET

EXPERTS MOVE AMONG LEVELS OF ABSTRACTION

Experts design their solutions at multiple levels of abstraction, concurrently. They know that focusing only on high-level models is likely to omit important detail and that working only on low-level code is likely to lead to inelegant solutions. In exploring a design solution, they deliberately move up and down among levels of abstraction, and use resonances among them to spark insights and identify problems.

47

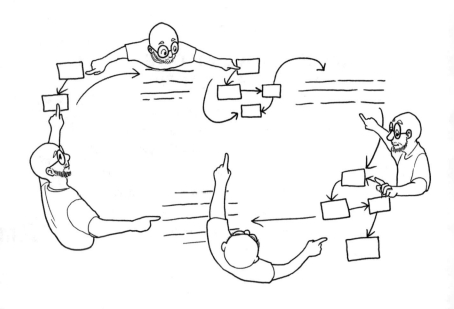

EXPERTS ROTATE AMONG SUBJECT PAIRS

Even in the throes of working on detailed issues concerning a design, experts iterate through issues in combination. They know that it is futile to consider a single issue in isolation for a long period of time. Rather, they juxtapose them: experts choose to focus on two (occasionally three) separate issues, consider them together, make some progress, and move on to the next pair of issues fairly quickly. In cycling through and iterating over pairs of issues, they ensure that different aspects of the design stay in sync with one another as they formulate the overall solution.

 48

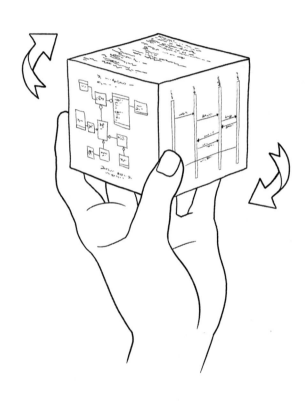

EXPERTS CHANGE NOTATION DELIBERATELY

Experts ask themselves what would happen if they remodeled what they have in a different notation, using somewhat different modeling concepts or somewhat different semantics. Differences in expression can prompt them to consider additional issues.

49

EXPERTS
PAUSE

Experts prefer to build discontinuity into the design process: by taking a break, they are more likely to uncover fresh issues the next time.

EXPERTS
TEST

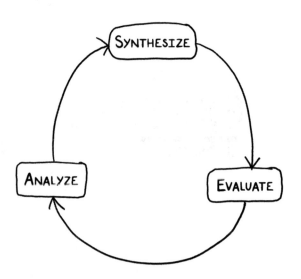

EXPERTS ARE SKEPTICAL

Where others are content, experts remain skeptical. They are skeptical that they explored the necessary breadth and depth of possible solutions. They are skeptical that the current leading solution is good, or even just good enough. They are skeptical of others', and their own, ideas. That is why they test their designs. Testing can provide instructive evidence: whether the design meets its objectives, whether there are emergent issues, or whether assumptions are justified.

EXPERTS SIMULATE CONTINUALLY

Experts imagine how a design will work—simulating aspects of the envisioned software and how the different parts of the design support a variety of scenarios. When working with others, experts regularly walk through a design by verbalizing its operation step-by-step. When alone, they simulate mentally, exercising the design repeatedly over time.

52

```
IF (CAR APPROACHES INTERSECTION)
  IF (INTERSECTION.LIGHT IS RED)
          CAR.SPEED = 0
  ELSE IF (INTERSECTION.LIGHT IS YELLOW)
          CAR.SPEED += 10
```

EXPERTS DRAW EXAMPLES ALONGSIDE THEIR DIAGRAMS

On their own, design diagrams remain passive abstractions. This is why experts draw examples alongside the diagrams when they simulate a design. Externalizing their thoughts, juxtaposing the simulation with their design, and envisioning the execution in context, forces them to interpret what they drew and to test their design more thoroughly in the process.

EXPERTS TEST ACROSS REPRESENTATIONS

Different aspects of a design solution are often represented in different diagrams—commonly in different notations altogether. Rather than testing each of these in isolation, experts know to juxtapose them in order to examine their dependencies, constraints, interactions, and other alignments.

54

EXPERTS PROTOTYPE CONCEPTS

Experts know that people struggle to engage with abstractions and therefore frequently turn to prototypes to elicit feedback. Prototypes, whether on paper or as more realistic mock-ups, show concretely how the proposed design will behave. They allow stakeholders to engage with and respond to the design concepts, potentially providing important contextual information.

55

EXPERTS
PLAY THE FOOL

Experts pretend to be ignorant, purposely setting aside
what they know about the design in order to expose
assumptions and flaws. Similarly, they place themselves
in the shoes of a novice user, or a co-worker
unfamiliar with the design, and imagine the questions
they would ask.

56

EXPERTS ARE ALERT TO EVIDENCE THAT CHALLENGES THEIR THEORY

Experts remain alert to anything that might challenge what they believe about their design. They are open to information that is unexpected, and are particularly sensitive to any indication that their design might be wrong. An offhand comment from a future user that does not align with the current design might well prompt a significant shift in design scope.

To experts, no issue is too small to investigate, for they know that small issues can be indicative of much larger problems lurking beneath the surface.

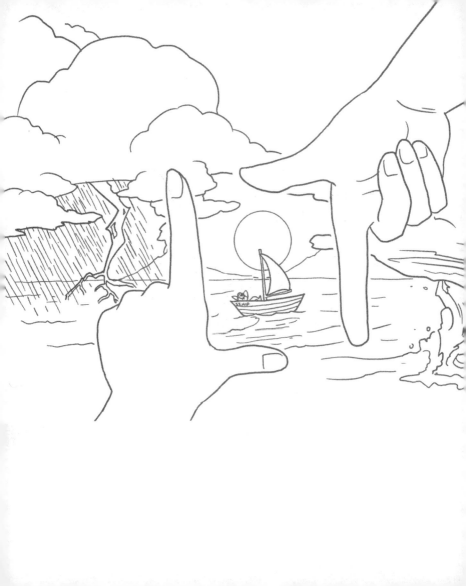

EXPERTS
REFLECT

EXPERTS CURTAIL DIGRESSIONS

It is not uncommon for designers to realize suddenly that they have been discussing an at-best marginal issue for half a meeting. Experts know that, in the midst of design, it is easy to lose sight of what is happening, and they make it a practice to check regularly where they are and where they are going. They use this information to abandon unproductive work, and focus effort where it needs to be focused.

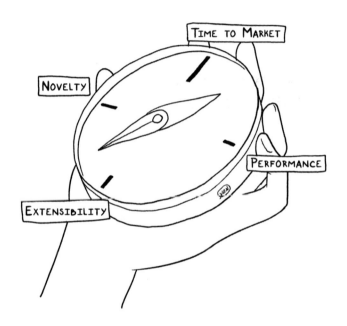

EXPERTS RETAIN THEIR ORIENTATION

After many meetings, changes, and enhancements, losing track of how the design at hand actually works is not unusual. Experts know the importance of understanding fully the essential underlying concepts of a design, and they make every effort to ensure that they remember the decisions that have already been made, the ones that still need to be made, and why this is so.

EXPERTS THINK ABOUT WHAT THEY ARE NOT DESIGNING

While it is natural to focus on what a design must accomplish, experts also spend time thinking about what a design is *not* intended to do. In articulating and considering boundaries, they discover where they are over- and under-designing.

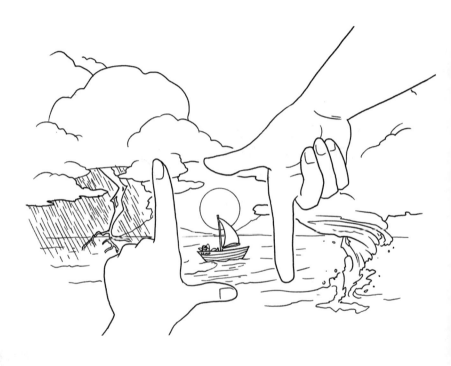

EXPERTS RE-ASSESS THE LANDSCAPE

Experts periodically step back, not just to examine progress, but also to reflect on the project as a whole. They question whether they are still solving the right problem. Have client goals changed? User perceptions? Technology? Deployment context? Market? Experts ask these questions with regularity, to ensure the software they design is fit for purpose.

EXPERTS INVEST NOW
TO SAVE EFFORT LATER

In reflecting on an ongoing design project, experts
also anticipate what issues might emerge later.
They foreshadow alternative futures, and perform
cost-benefit analyses to determine whether
investments now—in methods, tools, resources, design
alternatives—could save effort later.

EXPERTS
KEEP GOING

EXPERTS DESIGN ALL THE TIME

Experts design at their desk, when taking a walk, on their way to work or back home, in the shower, in the gym, and anywhere else—including in design meetings and conversations. They mull over a design whenever and wherever they can—through habit or preoccupation—as they know that inspiration can strike at any moment.

EXPERTS KNOW DESIGN IS NOT DONE UNTIL THE CODE IS DELIVERED AND RUNNING

The success of a design is determined largely by the experiences of the users. Experts know that any design decision can drastically influence perceptions. They do not consider their designs done until the code is delivered and running. That is when the users finally experience the software.

64

EXPERTS
KEEP LEARNING

Experts do not take their expertise for granted. They are continuously on the lookout for new knowledge to add to their repertoire, and they explicitly seek out and make time for opportunities to learn.

EXPERTS
PLAY

Experts play with new hardware and new programming languages. They play with toys and technology of all kinds. They play with mathematical and logical problems. They play with random new design challenges they make up for themselves. Play is invigorating; it helps keep their minds fresh, exposes them to novel designs, prompts them to reflect on classic designs, and opens their minds to invention and imagination.

AUTHOR BIOS